GRADE
5

Success With

Math

SCHOLASTIC

Scholastic Inc. grants teachers permission to photocopy the reproducible pages from this book for classroom use.
No other part of this publication may be reproduced in whole or in part, or stored in a retrieval system,
or transmitted in any form or by any means, electronic, mechanical, photocopying,
recording, or otherwise without written permission of the publisher. For information regarding
permission, write to Scholastic Inc., 557 Broadway, New York, NY 10012.

Editor: Ourania Papacharalambous
Cover design by Tannaz Fassihi; cover illustration by Kevin Zimmer
Interior design by Cynthia Ng
Interior illustrations by Doug Jones (5, 13, 17, 20, 22, 26–29, 31–32, 35, 44)
All other images @ Shutterstock.com

ISBN 978-1-338-79853-1
Scholastic Inc., 557 Broadway, New York, NY 10012
Copyright © 2022 Scholastic Inc.
All rights reserved. Printed in the U.S.A.
First printing, January 2022
1 2 3 4 5 6 7 8 9 10   40   29 28 27 26 25 24 23 22

INTRODUCTION

Parents and teachers alike will find *Scholastic Success With Math* to be a valuable educational tool. It is designed to help students in the fifth grade improve their math skills. The practice pages incorporate challenging puzzles, inviting games, and picture problems that students are sure to enjoy. On page 4, you will find a list of the key skills covered in the activities throughout this book. Students will practice skills such as basic operations and computations, multiplication, division, fractions, decimals, and much more! They are also challenged to measure length, compare units of measure, identify fractions, and tell time. Remember to praise students for their efforts and successes!

TABLE OF CONTENTS

Grade-Appropriate Skills Covered in *Scholastic Success With Math: Grade 5*

Write simple expressions that record calculations with numbers and interpret numerical expressions without evaluating them.

Generate two numerical patterns using two given rules. Identify apparent relationships between corresponding terms.

Fluently multiply multi-digit whole numbers using the standard algorithm.

Find whole-number quotients of whole numbers with up to four-digit dividends and two-digit divisors, using strategies based on place value, the properties of operations, and/or the relationship between multiplication and division.

Interpret a fraction as division of the numerator by the denominator ($a/b = a \div b$). Solve word problems involving division of whole numbers leading to answers in the form of fractions or mixed numbers.

Convert among different-sized standard measurement units within a given measurement system (e.g., convert 5 cm to 0.05 m), and use these conversations in solving multi-step, real world problems.

Recognize volume as an attribute of solid figures and understand concepts of volume and measurement.

Relate volume to the operations of multiplication and addition and solve real world and mathematical problems involving volume.

Use a pair of perpendicular number lines, called axes, to define a coordinate system, with the intersection of the lines (the origin) arranged to coincide with the 0 on each line and a given point in the plane located by using an ordered pair of numbers, called its coordinates. Understand that the first number indicates how far to travel from the origin in the direction of one axis, and the second number indicates how far to travel in the direction of one axis, with the convention that the names of the two axes and the coordinates correspond.

What's in a Word?

A prefix is a word part added at the beginning of a word. A prefix changes the meaning of a word. The prefixes in this activity help form words that represent numbers. Each statement contains a word with a number prefix. The list below contains numbers written out as words. Fill each blank with the correct word from the list below.

> nine   ten   hundred   three   two   eight   one   thousand

1. An animal with _____ horn on its head is called a **uni**corn.

2. A **dec**ade lasts _____ years.

3. An **oct**opus has _____ tentacles.

4. A **tri**athlete participates in _____ Olympic events.

5. A **bi**cycle has _____ wheels.

6. A **cent**ury marks a _____ years.

7. A **non**agon is a shape with _____ sides.

8. A **kilo**meter is equal to a _____ meters.

⭐ Research other number prefixes. Try finding some that represent larger numbers. Share them with your classmates.

A Stinky Riddle

Answer each question.

To solve the riddle, find the question number at the bottom of the page.

Then, use your answers and the Decoder to fill in the blanks.

1 In the number 52,370, the digit 2 is in which place? _____

2 In the number 619,246, which digit is in the hundred thousands place? _____

3 In the number 2,027,635, the digit 3 is in which place? _____

4 In the number 37,196,511, which digit is in the millions place? _____

5 In the number 402,819,335, which digit is in the ten millions place? _____

6 In the number 9,817,248,100, which place is the digit 9 in? _____

7 In the number 6,543,210,789, which place is the digit 5 in? _____

8 Which number is greater: 727,912 or 699,534? _____

9 Which number is smaller: 4,847,266 or 5,000,122? _____

10 Which number is greater: 7,446,726,012 or 7,446,732,011? _____

Decoder

7,446,726,012	K
ones	P
1	W
4,847,266	T
7	N
thousands	I
699,534	A
hundreds	O
7,446,732,011	T
billions	R
tens	S
ten millions	B
6	E
5,000,122	D
ten thousands	V
0	E
hundred millions	M
9	F
5	H
727,912	E

How do skunks measure length?

IN "SC___ ___ ___" ___ ___ ___ ___ ___ ___ ___
     8 4 9   1 7 5 10 2 6 3

Now That's Talent!

Figure it out!

1 Using RIBBIT and CROAK, a frog can make these 2-word phrases: RIBBIT-CROAK and CROAK-RIBBIT. What 2-word phrases can a dog make of BARK and RUFF? (Use each word only once in each phrase.)

_____

2 How many different 2-word phrases can a dog make out of the words BARK and GRR? Write each arrangement.

_____

3 How many different 2-word phrases can a cat make out of the words MEOW, PURR, and SSS? Write each arrangement.

_____

4 How many different 3-word phrases can a cat make out of the words MEOW, PURR, and SSS? Write each arrangement.

_____

Cow Rounding

Round each number.
To solve the riddle, find the
question number at the bottom
of the page. Then, use your
answers and the Decoder to
fill in the blanks.

1 Round 789 to the nearest hundred. _____

2 Round 5,112 to the nearest thousand. _____

3 Round 3,660 to the nearest hundred. _____

4 Round 1,499 to the nearest thousand. _____

5 Round 2,771 to the nearest ten. _____

6 Round 7,529 to the nearest thousand. _____

7 Round 24,397 to the nearest hundred. _____

8 Round 10,708 to the nearest thousand. _____

9 Round 9,937 to the nearest ten. _____

10 Round 73,489 to the nearest thousand. _____

Decoder

700	F
11,000	K
800	S
2,780	O
3,600	U
1,000	M
9,900	Y
24,400	I
73,000	S
5,000	L
24,000	P
6,000	Q
2,770	E
7,500	T
9,940	A
3,700	K
10,000	R
8,000	H
2,000	N

What do cows give after an earthquake?

___ ___ ___ ___   ___ ___ ___ ___ ___ ___
 4   7   2   8   10   6   9   3   5   1

Apple Add-Up Game

Materials:
- small counters
- pencil
- paper cup

OBJECT: To cover more apples than the other player.

NUMBER OF PLAYERS: 2

TO PLAY:

- Each player gets a copy of the apple tree game board. Decide who will go first.

- Take turns spinning. (Look at the picture to see how to use the spinner.) After spinning, cover two apples on your tree with the counters. The two numbers on the apples must add up to a number that matches the spinner. Example: Player 1 spins "Equal to 15." Player 1 can cover 7 and 8, 5 and 10, 2 and 13, or any other combination of two apples that totals 15. Player 2 spins "More than 15." Player 2 can cover any combination of two apples that totals more than 15.

- Once your counters are on the board, you can't move them!

- If you can't cover two apples to match the spinner, you're out. The other player wins.

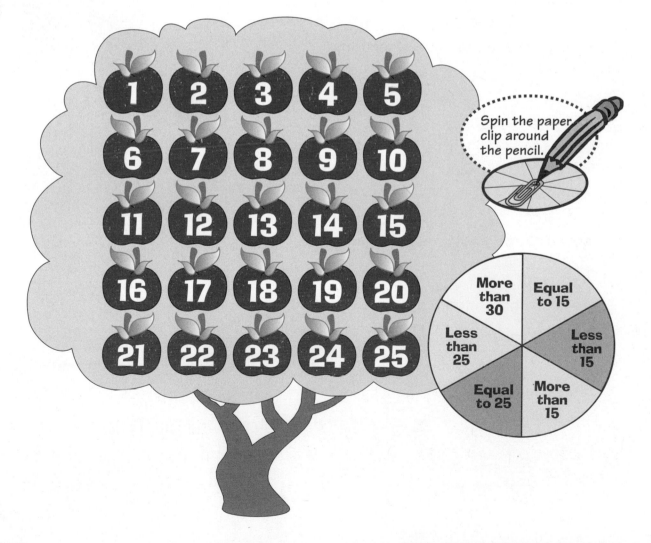

Spin the paper clip around the pencil.

A World of Averages

What's an average? It's a number that describes a group of numbers. It isn't the biggest number in the group, or the smallest. It's somewhere in between. For example, the average number of people that visit one park each day is about 77,000.

That doesn't mean that exactly 77,000 people visit that park every day. Some days, more than 77,000 people visit. Other days, fewer than 77,000 people visit. But 77,000—the average—is about how many people visit on most days.

> To find the average of any set of numbers, add all the numbers. Then, divide the total by the number of numbers in the set.

Finding an Average

Say you went on a three-day trip. How could you find the average number of hours you walked each day? Here's one way:
Add up the actual number of hours you walked each day.

10 hours + 8 hours + 6 hours = 24 hours

Then, divide the total by the number of days you added up.

24 hours ÷ 3 days = 8 hours

You walked an average of 8 hours each day.

Find the average of each set of numbers to learn more about what happens on an "average" day at this park.

1 25 and 175

About _____ pairs of sunglasses are turned in to the Lost and Found in the park every day.

2 5,000 and 7,000

You can choose from about _____ different food items.

3 881; 924; and 1,234

About _____ baseball caps are sold.

4 3,259; 4,039; and 5,443

About _____ T-shirts are bought.

5 10,660; 28,069; 58,392; and 78,223

About _____ packets of ketchup are handed out.

6 5,400; 10,000; 11,608; and 33,124

About _____ hamburgers are sold.

7 117; 3,274; 15,673; and 41,208

About _____ pounds of potatoes are used to make french fries.

8 35; 126; 780; 1,050; and 3,009

About _____ bandages are given out.

All Mixed Up

Finding the sum is easy. But when you try to put these numbers correctly in the puzzle, you'll find yourself all mixed up!

(puzzle grid with cells reading 1, 5, 2)

Find the sum and write the answer in the puzzle. Each digit can occupy only one place to make the whole puzzle fit together perfectly. The first one has been done for you.

54 + 98 **152**	69 + 37	31 + 85	292 + 614	589 + 92	261 + 97
423 + 79	180 + 98	349 + 301	2,012 + 2,106	413 + 923	855 + 723
1,617 + 1,281	4,068 + 784	1,602 + 639	5,142 + 2,690	1,069 + 1,103	1,597 + 346
4,115 + 106	1,022 + 1,886	951 + 1,384	12,401 + 6,001	44,595 + 13,816	5,354 + 1,346

A Riddle to Grow On

Subtract.
To solve the riddle, find the question number at the bottom of the page. Then, use your answers and the Decoder to fill in the blanks.

1. 714 – 457 = _____

2. 936 – 508 = _____

3. 1,000 – 700 = _____

4. 1,362 – 619 = _____

5. 2,000 – 549 = _____

6. 3,873 – 1,004 = _____

7. 1,446 – 987 = _____

8. 5,011 – 4,963 = _____

9. 8,600 – 3,716 = _____

10. 9,925 – 1,999 = _____

Decoder

4,884	T
64	C
275	D
459	V
286	W
1,451	B
257	L
1,541	K
428	G
81	M
743	E
48	E
792	P
2,869	S
12	Z
300	E
2,942	Y
7,926	A
7,431	Q

What tables grow on farms?

" ___ ___ ___ ___   ___ ___ ___ ___ ___ ___ "
  7   4   2   8   9 10   5   1   3   6

Mystery Multiplication & Division

Using the digits in the box, write the answer to each number riddle in the form of an equation. Digits appear only once in an answer.

$$8 \quad 1 \quad 4 \quad 7 \quad 3$$

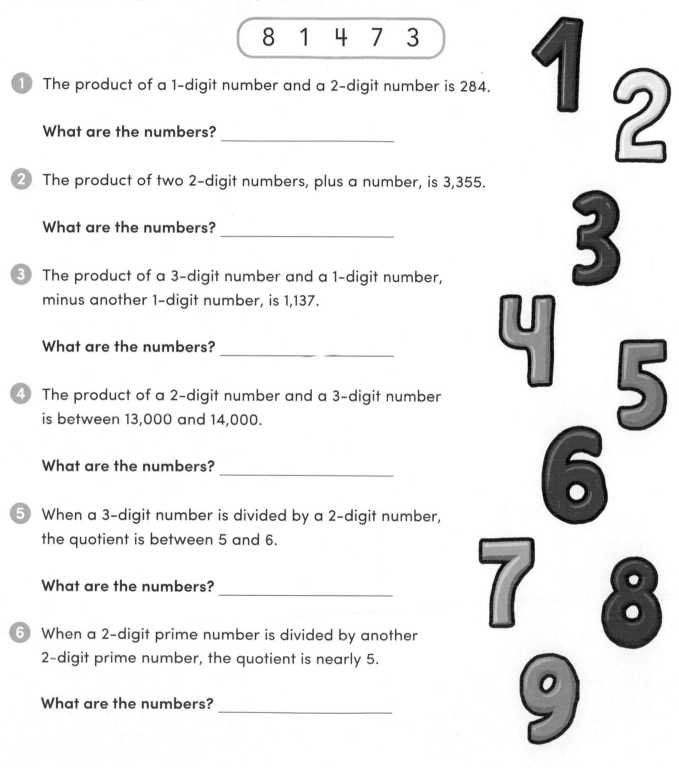

1 The product of a 1-digit number and a 2-digit number is 284.

What are the numbers? _____

2 The product of two 2-digit numbers, plus a number, is 3,355.

What are the numbers? _____

3 The product of a 3-digit number and a 1-digit number, minus another 1-digit number, is 1,137.

What are the numbers? _____

4 The product of a 2-digit number and a 3-digit number is between 13,000 and 14,000.

What are the numbers? _____

5 When a 3-digit number is divided by a 2-digit number, the quotient is between 5 and 6.

What are the numbers? _____

6 When a 2-digit prime number is divided by another 2-digit prime number, the quotient is nearly 5.

What are the numbers? _____

A "Barber"ous Riddle

Multiply.
To solve the riddle, find the question number at the bottom of the page. Then, use your answers and the Decoder to fill in the blanks.

1 $1 \times 2 \times 3 =$ _____

2 $2 \times 4 \times 1 =$ _____

3 $5 \times 3 \times 4 =$ _____

4 $3 \times 7 \times 3 =$ _____

5 $8 \times 4 \times 5 =$ _____

6 $6 \times 6 \times 7 =$ _____

7 $9 \times 2 \times 5 =$ _____

8 $1 \times 8 \times 7 =$ _____

9 $7 \times 9 \times 5 =$ _____

10 $4 \times 6 \times 4 =$ _____

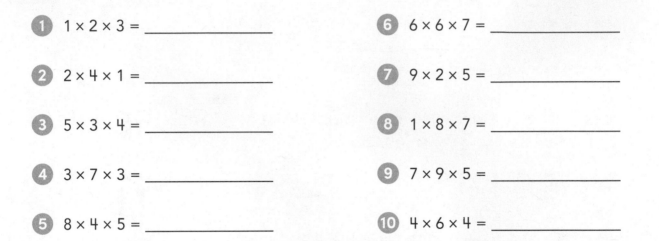

Key

150	V	315	N	225	A
8	E	252	O	63	E
84	K	6	B	90	D
56	W	351	Z	60	T
160	H	96	T	57	X

How did the detective find the missing barber?

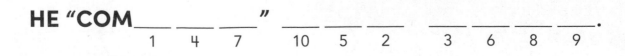

HE "COM___ ___ ___" ___ ___ ___ ___ ___ ___ ___.
      1 4 7   10 5 2   3 6 8 9

Fact Search

The puzzle below has many hidden multiplication number sentences.
You'll find number sentences going across, up and down, and
at an angle. Most number sentences overlap. Circle each
multiplication number sentence you find. Happy searching!

6	5	0	70	2	1	8	8	64
8	0	7	1	6	12	1	7	7
48	10	0	3	4	7	8	56	6
90	10	9	3	7	21	42	21	7
9	100	5	16	28	5	7	35	42
2	4	8	50	8	3	24	5	3
20	2	40	10	4	6	6	36	35
4	6	80	2	32	18	9	18	4
7	7	49	20	5	4	54	9	6
11	42	28	2	8	10	36	2	24

Caught in the Web

Multiply.
To solve the riddle, find the question number at the bottom of the page. Then, use your answers and the Decoder to fill in the blanks.

1. 1,000 × 11 = _____

2. 2,000 × 12 = _____

3. 3,000 × 10 = _____

4. 4,000 × 14 = _____

5. 5,000 × 20 = _____

6. 6,000 × 24 = _____

7. 7,000 × 30 = _____

8. 8,000 × 32 = _____

9. 9,000 × 40 = _____

10. 7,500 × 50 = _____

Key

56,000.............. H	65,000..............M	30,000.............. C
11,000 I	144,000 ....T	375,000............ C
265,000............B	25,000.............. N	10,000 ....Y
360,000............F	256,000............ L	100,000 ....A
210,000 ....E	90,000..............Q	24,000..............S

Why did the spider join the baseball team?

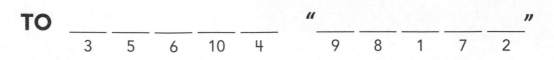

TO ___ ___ ___ ___ ___ " ___ ___ ___ ___ ___ "
     3   5   6   10   4   9   8   1   7   2

Face Facts

The most common way people recognize each other is by the way they look. Each person has distinct eyes, ears, and other features that set them apart from everyone else. Try answering the wacky riddle below to name another feature people have that sets them apart. Factors will help you find the answer.

Each number is followed by two possible factors. Circle the letter after the number that is a factor. Write the letters in order from the first problem to the last to solve the riddle.

1	22	2 I	6 **O**
2	70	5 **T**	15 A
3	48	5 O	8 **S**
4	80	16 **T**	11 B
5	120	3 **U**	13 E
6	644	9 D	7 **L**
7	182	13 **I**	4 L
8	156	16 F	4 **P**
9	198	10 R	9 **S**

What grows between your nose and your chin?

__ __ ' __ " __ __ __ __ __ __ __ __ "!

Make a list of numbers on another sheet of paper. Ask a classmate to find at least two factors for each number.

Bug Out!

Find each quotient.
**To solve the riddle, find the question number
at the bottom of the page. Then, use your
answers and the Decoder to fill in the blanks.**

1 74 ÷ 5 = _____

2 26 ÷ 9 = _____

3 41 ÷ 4 = _____

4 55 ÷ 10 = _____

5 37 ÷ 14 = _____

6 66 ÷ 22 = _____

7 84 ÷ 17 = _____

8 100 ÷ 11 = _____

9 128 ÷ 32 = _____

10 200 ÷ 25 = _____

Decoder

14 remainder 4 ... M
4 remainder 16 L
5 .... P
6 ....O
9 remainder 1 ...... E
10 remainder 1..... A
5 remainder 5...... T
14 remainder 3 .... K
9 remainder 3...... S
4 L
7...............................C
2 remainder 8...... S
4 remainder 15 .... N
8 .... E
10 remainder 4 ....D
12 remainder 2..... U
2 remainder 9...... A
5 remainder 6...... R
3............................. B

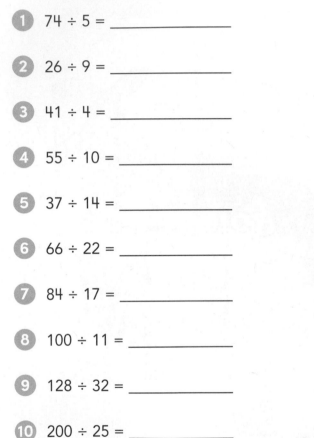

What has 18 legs and catches flies?

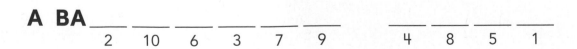

A BA___ ___ ___ ___ ___ ___   ___ ___ ___ ___
      2   10   6   3   7   9   4   8   5   1

What Number Am I?

Write the answer to each number riddle in the form of an equation. Digits appear only once in an answer.

1   I am a 2-digit number. The sum of my digits is 11. I am divisible by both 4 and 7.

    What number am I? _____

2   I am a 2-digit number divisible by 4, 6, and 7.

    What number am I? _____

3   I am a 2-digit number divisible by 19. The sum of my digits is 14.

    What number am I? _____

4   I am a 3-digit number divisible by 7, but not 2. The sum of my digits is 4.

    What number am I? _____

5   I am a 3-digit number less than 300. I am divisible by 2 and 5, but not 3. The sum of my digits is 7.

    What number am I? _____

6   I am a 3-digit number divisible by 3. My tens digit is 3 times as great as my hundreds digit, and the sum of my digits is 15. If you reverse my digits, I am divisible by 6, as well as by 3.

    What number am I? _____

Running Riddle

Find each quotient.
To solve the riddle, find the question number at the bottom of the page. Then, use your answers and the Decoder to fill in the blanks.

1 100 ÷ 25 = _____

2 330 ÷ 16 = _____

3 407 ÷ 37 = _____

4 562 ÷ 84 = _____

5 646 ÷ 71 = _____

6 950 ÷ 100 = _____

7 1,000 ÷ 200 = _____

8 1,200 ÷ 36 = _____

9 1,540 ÷ 50 = _____

10 2,003 ÷ 66 = _____

Decoder
20 remainder 10.....R
8 ....B
30 remainder 40....A
7 remainder 9 ....F
11................................K
6 remainder 56 ......E
40 remainder 30...O
4 ....T
12 ....M
33 remainder 12 I
32 remainder 12 L
9 remainder 7 ....Y
8 remainder 50 ..... N
30 remainder 23 ... D
9 remainder 50 C
6 remainder 58 ......S
5 remainder 2 ....Q
6 ....W
5 ....A

What has 3 feet but can't run?

___ ___ ___ ___ ___ ___ ___ ___ ___ ___
 7   5   9   2   10 4   1   8   6   3

The Squirm-ulator

Figure it out!

1   Help out Squirmy Worm. What do you get when you multiply 6 by 7, then subtract 13? Use a calculator to check the answer.

_____

2   Squirmy multiplies 8 by 5, then divides the product by 4. What is the answer?

_____

3   Moovis the Cow multiplies 11 by 14. Then, she divides the product by 7. What is the answer?

_____

4   Multiply the number of days there are in a week by 12. Subtract 24. What is the answer?

_____

5   How old are you? Multiply your age in years by 17. Then, add or subtract to get a total of 200. What number did you add or subtract?

_____

Number Stumper

Put ÷, ×, +, or – in the boxes to make correct math sentences.

1

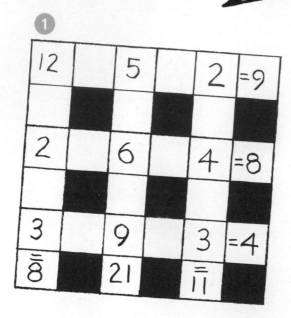

2

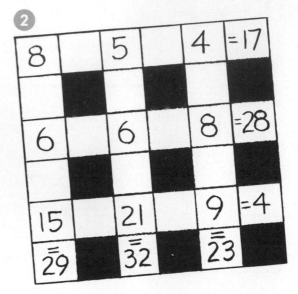

3

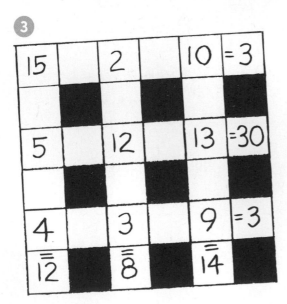

4

Magnetic Math

Subtract.

To solve the riddle, find the question number at the bottom of the page. Then, use your answers and the Decoder to fill in the blanks.

1 $\dfrac{2}{3} - \dfrac{1}{3} =$ _____

2 $\dfrac{5}{8} - \dfrac{2}{8} =$ _____

3 $\dfrac{7}{11} - \dfrac{4}{11} =$ _____

4 $\dfrac{19}{20} - \dfrac{5}{20} =$ _____

5 $\dfrac{27}{32} - \dfrac{20}{32} - \dfrac{6}{32} =$ _____

6 $\dfrac{42}{67} - \dfrac{18}{67} - \dfrac{4}{67} =$ _____

7 $\dfrac{79}{83} - \dfrac{11}{83} - \dfrac{9}{83} =$ _____

8 $\dfrac{100}{121} - \dfrac{78}{121} =$ _____

9 $\dfrac{44}{156} - \dfrac{29}{156} - \dfrac{12}{156} =$ _____

10 $\dfrac{247}{312} - \dfrac{59}{312} - \dfrac{39}{312} - \dfrac{50}{312} =$ _____

Decoder

1/3	T
3/165	V
1/32	A
15/20	B
21/67	F
99/312	T
61/83	K
59/83	U
4/156	L
3/8	C
11/121	W
3/11	A
22/121	T
2/32	I
4/11	U
14/20	R
3/12	N
20/67	M
3/156	E

What did one magnet say to the other magnet?

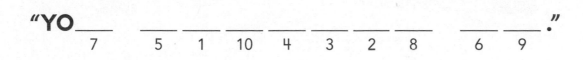

"YO___ ___ ___ ___ ___ ___ ___ ___ ___ ___."
　　7　　　5　1　10　4　3　2　8　　6　9

Everyone Needs Math!

Multiply.

To solve the riddle, find the question number at the bottom of the page. Then, use your answers and the Decoder to fill in the blanks.

1 $3 \times \dfrac{1}{2} =$ _____

2 $5 \times \dfrac{1}{3} =$ _____

3 $2 \times \dfrac{1}{6} =$ _____

4 $4 \times \dfrac{2}{5} =$ _____

5 $3 \times \dfrac{3}{4} =$ _____

6 $2 \times \dfrac{7}{8} =$ _____

7 $6 \times \dfrac{6}{9} =$ _____

8 $5 \times \dfrac{2}{3} =$ _____

9 $4 \times \dfrac{4}{7} =$ _____

10 $6 \times \dfrac{9}{11} =$ _____

Key

3/2.................M	45/11.................F	10/3 ....E
16/7 ....Y	9/4.................D	8/7.................G
6/3.................W	2/3.................Z	36/9 ....R
2/6................. N	54/11.................U	8/5 ....S
14/8 ....B	3/6.................T	5/3.................B

Why did the artist need math?

HE PAINTE ___ ___ ___ ___ ___ ___ ___ ___ ___ ___ ___ .
$\quad\quad\quad$ 5 $\quad$ 2 $\quad$ 9 $\quad$ 3 $\quad$ 10 $\quad$ 1 $\quad$ 6 $\quad$ 8 $\quad$ 7 $\quad$ 4

Fruity Fractions

To change a fraction to a decimal, follow these steps.

1. First, reduce the fraction to lowest terms.

$$\frac{20}{4000} = \frac{1}{200}$$

2. Then, divide the numerator by the denominator. Add a decimal point and a zero.

$$200 \overline{)1} \qquad 200 \overline{)\overset{0.}{1.000}}$$

3. Finally, subtract.

$$200 \overline{)\overset{0.005}{1.000}} \qquad \frac{20}{4000} = 0.005$$

$$\begin{array}{r} -\ 0 \downarrow \\ \hline 10 \\ -\ 0 \downarrow \\ \hline 100 \\ -\ 0 \downarrow \\ \hline 1000 \\ -1000 \\ \hline 0 \end{array}$$

One way to answer the tricky riddle below, Why does a banana use suntan lotion?, is to turn the fractions into equivalent decimals. There are two answers after each problem. Circle the letter after the correct answer. When you're done, write the circled letters in order from the first problem to the last in the blank spaces below. Note: The answer choices below are rounded.

1	6/10	0.6	**S**	0.1	**T**	**9**	16/5	6.2	**D**	3.2	**P**
2	4/9	3.2	**L**	0.4	**O**	**10**	3/4	5.7	**U**	0.75	**E**
3	42/100	4.20	**A**	0.42	**I**	**11**	14/3	4.6	**E**	9.3	**A**
4	13/5	2.6	**T**	5.3	**M**	**12**	8/1,000	0.008	**L**	0.08	**R**
5	8/3	2.6	**W**	7.4	**B**						
6	11/50	0.22	**O**	2.12	**E**						
7	5/20	.025	**I**	0.25	**N**						
8	7/100	0.07	**T**	7.10	**B**						

Why does a banana use suntan lotion?

___ ___ ___ ___ ___ ___ ___ , ___ ___ ___ ___ ___ .

Decimals Around the Diamond

The numbers after a decimal point are always between 0 and 1. They are written to the right of the ones place. Decimals always have a decimal point to the left of them.

.325

decimal point | tenths place | hundredths place | thousandths place

Baseball fans always argue about who's the best player. Everybody seems to have a favorite! When it comes to finding the best hitter, though, no one can argue with batting averages. The batting average shows how often a baseball player gets a hit. It is a 3-digit decimal number, and it looks like this: .328, .287, .311, .253. The larger the batting average is, the better the hitter is.

Read the chart of baseball players' batting averages from 2015. Rank the batting averages. This means number the batting averages in order from highest to lowest. (See Home Plate for help.) Write the numbers 1 to 10 in the boxes next to the names—1 for the highest average, 10 for the lowest. Ready? Play ball!

HOME PLATE

To rank decimal numbers:
• Start at the left.
• Compare the digits in the same place.
• Find the first place where the digits are different.
• The number with the smaller digit is the smaller number. Example: Rank .317 and . 312

.317
↑↑↑
.312

So .312 is smaller than .317.

Rank	Player (Team)	2015 Batting Average
	Yunel Escobar (Washington Nationals)	.314
	A. J. Pollock (Arizona Diamondbacks)	.315
	Buster Posey (San Francisco Giants)	.318
	Bryce Harper (Washington Nationals)	.330
	Paul Goldschmidt (Arizona Diamondbacks)	.321
	Miguel Cabrera (Detroit Tigers)	.338
	Joey Votto (Cincinnati Reds)	.314
	Dee Strange-Gordon (Miami Marlins)	.333
	Xander Bogaerts (Boston Red Sox)	.320
	José Altuve (Houston Astros)	.313

Home Improvement?

Michelle's family just bought a new house. Workers were putting a few last-minute touches on it before the family moved in. But the day turned into one big disaster! Michelle will tell you all about it.

To complete Michelle's story, solve the problem next to each worker's name. Next, find your answer below a blank in the story. Write that worker's name in the blank. When you're done, read Michelle's story.

WORKER'S NAMES

1. 5% of 60 = _____ **Paul Plumber**

2. 50% of 1000 = _____ **Robert Roofer**

3. 6% of 450 = _____ **Penny Painter**

4. 8% of 90 = _____ **Alan Architect**

5. 40% of 200 = _____ **Gilbert Gardener**

6. 30% of 620 = _____ **Elway Electrician**

7. 20% of 100 = _____ **Carlton Carpenter**

MICHELLE'S STORY

I'll never forget the day the workers showed up at our new house! First,

_____ dropped his screwdriver on the floor. Then, _____

186
7.2

slipped on it and accidentally knocked a can of paint onto _____'s

20

diagrams. He was pretty upset about it and asked _____ to drive him

3

to pick up new ones. While they were pulling out of the driveway, they ran over

_____'s tools. _____ yelled for them to stop, but they

500
80

didn't hear him. _____ looked at all of this in disbelief. And so did I!

27

The Next Number . . .

Sometimes sets of numbers have something in common. They follow a pattern. Take a look at the numbers 4, 6, 8, and 10. As the pattern continues, each number gets larger by 2. Try completing the number patterns in the problems below. Some are tougher to figure out than others. Give 'em a try. Good luck! Use the space below and to the right to work out the problems.

1 8, 11, 14, 17, 20, _____, _____, _____

2 27, 29, 31, 33, 35, _____, _____, _____

3 2, 7, 12, 17, 22, 27, _____, _____, _____

4 5, 9, 14, 23, 37, 60, _____, _____, _____

5 39, 46, 53, 60, 67, 74, _____, _____, _____

6 6, 7, 13, 20, 33, 53, _____, _____, _____

7 4, 15, 26, 37, 48, _____, _____, _____

8 93, 116, 209, 325, 534, 859, _____, _____, _____

 On another sheet of paper, come up with several number patterns of your own. Ask someone to complete the patterns.

Times Terms

Write the multiplication word that fits each clue in the box. When you finish, copy the letters in the shaded boxes. Unscramble these letters to form another multiplication word.

1. Any number multiplied by this number comes out 0. ☐☐☐☐

2. Another word for "multiplied by" is _____. ☐☐☐☐☐

3. This is one of the numbers you multiply. ☐☐☐☐☐☐

4. Multiply a number by 3, and you _____ that number. ☐☐☐☐☐☐

5. Multiply a number by 2 to get the same answer as adding a _____. ☐☐☐☐☐☐

6. The answer when you multiply is called the _____. ☐☐☐☐☐☐☐

7. Its math symbol is ×: _____. ☐☐☐☐☐☐☐

8. Multiplication is the same as repeated _____. ☐☐☐☐☐☐☐☐

9. You can multiply if you have groups that are the _____ _____ (2 words). ☐☐☐☐ ☐☐☐☐

Write the letters from the shaded boxes here.

☐☐☐☐☐☐☐☐☐

Now unscramble them to make another word.

☐☐☐☐☐☐☐☐

Tell what this word means. _____

_____

_____

8 × 3 = 24
6 × 7 = 42

Mixed Operations

Write the answer to each number riddle below.

1. The sum of one-half of a number and one-fourth of 96 is 30.

   What is the number? _____

2. If you triple a number you will have one-half the number of hours in two days.

   What is the number? _____

3. If you double a number, you will get the same as the triple of one-fourth of 24.

   What is the number? _____

4. If you subtract a number from the square of 7 you will get one-fourth the product of 9 and 8.

   What is the number? _____

5. One-fifth of a number, subtracted from 20, is the same as one-fourth of 32.

   What is the number? _____

6. Think of two numbers whose greatest common factor is 12. If you divide the lesser of the two numbers by that greatest common factor, you get one-sixteenth of the other number.

   What are the numbers? _____

What a Sale!

There's a big sale over at the Clothing Coop. Ashley and Deondra are there to buy a few things. "How will we know how much money we're saving on each item?" Deondra asked. "Say a jacket that costs $32.00 has a sale tag that says 20% off," Ashley explained. "That means the store will take $ .20 off each dollar. In other words, the store will take a total of $6.40 off the original price of the jacket."

Help the girls figure out how much money the store will take off the other items they want to buy.

DOING THE MATH:
20 PERCENT OFF $32.00

Multiply the same way you would with whole numbers.

$32.00
x$ .20
64000

Add the number of decimal places.

$32.00
x$ .20
64000

4 decimal places altogether.

Move the decimal point 4 places to the left.

$32.00
x$ .20
6.4000

ANSWER
$6.40

1. What amount should be taken off the original price? _____

   What price will the girls pay for the pants? _____

2. How much should be taken off the original price? _____

   What will they pay for the blouse? _____

3. What amount should be taken off the original price? _____

   What's the sale price of the pocketbook? _____

4. How much should they take off the original price? _____

   What's the sale price of the shoes? _____

$17.00 40%

$24.00 30%

$22.00 15%

$65.00 20%

Multiplying & Dividing

Choose one number from the triangle and one from the circle to answer each question.

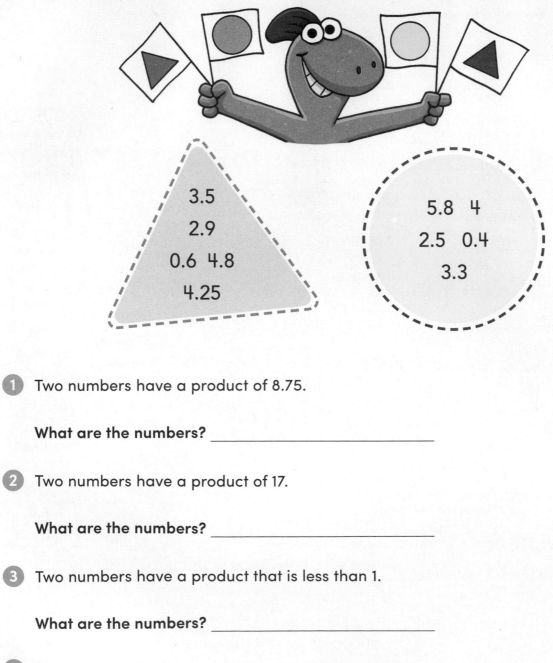

1 Two numbers have a product of 8.75.

What are the numbers? _____

2 Two numbers have a product of 17.

What are the numbers? _____

3 Two numbers have a product that is less than 1.

What are the numbers? _____

4 Two numbers have a product that is greater than 25.

What are the numbers? _____

Changing Shapes

Answer each question.

To solve the riddle, find the question number at the bottom of the page. Then, use your answers and the Decoder to fill in the blanks.

1 Joe has 2 apples. Tim has 2 times as many apples as Joe. How many apples does Tim have? _____

2 Kendra has 3 books. Paula has 3 times as many books as Kendra. How many books does Paula have? _____

3 Cliff has 5 times as many baseball caps as Wayne. Wayne has 5 baseball caps. How many baseball caps does Cliff have? _____

4 Jorge has 10 oranges. Wendy has 2 times as many oranges as Jorge. How many oranges does Wendy have? _____

5 Martha has 6 times as many coats as Russell. Russell has 5 coats. How many coats does Martha have? _____

6 Debbie has 9 pairs of shoes. How many shoes does she have in all? _____

7 Michael has 8 bunches of bananas. Each bunch has 7 bananas. How many bananas does he have in all? _____

8 Leroy has 11 times as many pencils as Renee. Renee has 11 pencils. How many pencils does Leroy have? _____

Key

4 apples	T
20 oranges	C
18 shoes	N
56 bananas	C
111 pencils	I
30 coats	U
2 apples	S
15 bananas	K
9 books	R
25 caps	R
121 pencils	O
40 coats	B

How did the square become a triangle?

IT ___ ___ ___ A ___ ___ ___ ___ E ___ .
    7   5   1   4   8   3   6   2

Weatherman

Figure it out!

1 Showers on Monday morning produced 0.5 inches of rain by noon. By 6 p.m., a total of 2 inches of rain had fallen. How many inches of rain fell between noon and 6 p.m.?

_____

2 On Tuesday, 1.2 inches of rain fell. Two more inches of rain fell the next day. How many

total inches of rain fell on both days? _____

3 The graph shows the high temperatures for Wednesday through Sunday. On which day was the highest temperature reached? The lowest? What was the difference between the two temperatures?

4 Between which two days did the temperature drop

15 degrees? Increase by 15 degrees? _____

5 Saturday's low temperature was 38°. How many degrees did the temperature rise to

reach Saturday's high temperature? _____

Volume Pops Up Everywhere!

Look around the room. Do you see any of the shapes shown here?

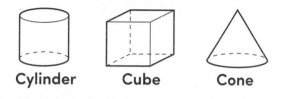

Cylinder   **Cube**   **Cone**

These shapes are 3-dimensional. That means that they are solid—you can touch them with your hands. (You can't hold a 2-dimensional shape like a circle, square, or triangle.) We measure 3-dimensional shapes in a special way—using volume. Volume tells how much the shape can hold inside.

Ready to learn about volume? Let's go!

1 Start with the cone and the yogurt cup. How many cones of popcorn do you think it will take to fill the yogurt cup?

_____ cones

Fill the cone with popcorn. Then, pour it into the cup. Keep filling the cup until you think it's half filled.
Do you want to change your guess?

New guess: _____ cones
Now finish filling the cup. How many cones did it take?

_____ cones

Materials:
- 2-lb bag of unpopped popcorn
- small ice cream cone
- empty 4-oz drink box with top cut off
- empty 8-oz yogurt cup
- 8- or 9-inch pie plate

2 How many cups of popcorn do you think it will take to fill the pie plate? Start pouring popcorn from the cup to the pie plate. When you think the pie plate is half filled, guess again. Then, fill it all the way. How many cups did it take?

_____ cups

3 Which do you think holds more, the cup or the drink box? How could you find out? Test your ideas. Which holds more?

_____

4 How many drink boxes of popcorn do you think it would take to fill the pie plate? Try it.

_____ drink boxes

Now pop the popcorn, fill the cone with ice cream, and have a volume party!

Get an "Angle" on Inventions

Everything that people use in their daily lives was invented by someone—things like the ironing board, the cash register, and ear muffs. In this activity, we ask you to match inventions like these to their inventor. Follow the directions below to get a new "angle" on a few famous inventions.

40°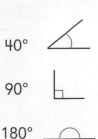

90°

180°

Follow these steps:

• Take a look at the angle that appears before each statement.

• Estimate the measure of the angle in degrees using the 40°, 90°, and 180° angles as a guide.

• Next, circle the name of the invention that appears next to the best estimate of that angle.

• Write the correct invention in the space provided in the statement.

11° hearing aid	90° ironing board	130° windshield wiper	160° cash register
80° ear muffs	175° railway signal	20° ballpoint pen	110° gas mask

1. The _____ was invented in 1888 by A. B. Blackburn.

2. S. Boone invented the _____ in 1892.

3. The _____ was invented in 1912 by Garrett A. Morgan.

4. The _____ was invented in 1879 by James Ritty.

5. In 1877, Chester Greenwood invented _____.

6. In 1935, Laszlo and Georg Biro established themselves as the first inventors of the _____.

7. In 1902, the _____ was invented by Miller Hutchison.

8. Other inventors expanded on her invention in later years. But Mary Anderson was the inventor of the first _____ in 1903.

Break the Ice With Perimeter and Area

Materials:
• square crackers or square counters

Jessie is building ice skating rinks for her friends. She measures the size of each rink in two ways—perimeter and area. Perimeter tells the measurement around the rink. Area tells how many square units fit inside each rink. Some rinks have the same area but different perimeters. Try building some yourself!

Here's the rink Jesse built for Shawn. Its area is 4. Its perimeter is 8.

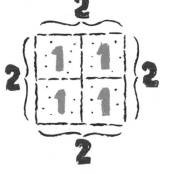

Use the square crackers to help you answer the questions. Then, draw how the crackers look.

1 Shawn wants a bigger rink. He wants it to have a perimeter of 12 and an area of 8. What can you add to Shawn's rink? Draw what it will look like.

2 Gil also wants a rink with a perimeter of 12. But he wants it to be square. What will it look like? What will its area be? Draw what it will look like.

3 The area of Rita's rink is 12. Its perimeter is 14. What does her rink look like? Draw it.

4 Sonia wants her rink to have an area of 16. She says it can be shaped like a square or a rectangle. What could the rink look like? What will its perimeter be? Draw it.

5 José wants a rink with an area of 24. It can be any shape. What are some of the shapes it could be? What are their perimeters? Draw one example.

Check This Out!

Answer each question.
To solve the riddle, find the question
number at the bottom of the page.
Then, use your answers and the Decoder
to fill in the blanks.

1 How many inches
   are there in 1 foot? _____

2 How many inches
   are there in 2 feet? _____

3 How many inches
   are there in 4 feet? _____

4 How many inches
   are there in 5 feet? _____

5 How many inches
   are there in 7 feet? _____

6 How many inches
   are there in 9 feet? _____

7 How many inches
   are there in 10 feet? _____

8 How many inches
   are there in 6 feet? _____

9 How many inches
   are there in 12 feet? _____

10 How many inches
    are there in 15 feet? _____

Key

60 ....E	72....................D	88 ....M
84 C	140..................I	64 ....P
180.................O	120..................H	12 ....U
100.................G	110...................L	24 ....K
108.................T	144..................E	48 C

Why did the sick book visit the library?

TO GET " ___ ___ ___ ___ ___ ___ ___   ___ ___ ___ "
         3   7   4   5   2   9   8   10 1   6

A Royal Riddle

Answer each question.
To solve the riddle, find the question number at the bottom of the page. Then, use your answers and the Decoder to fill in the blanks.

1 How many minutes are there in 1 hour? _____

2 How many minutes are there in 2 hours? _____

3 How many minutes are there in 4 hours? _____

4 How many minutes are there in 5 hours? _____

5 How many minutes are there in 7 hours? _____

6 How many minutes are there in 10 hours? _____

7 How many minutes are there in 11 hours? _____

8 How many minutes are there in 15 hours? _____

9 How many minutes are there in 18 hours? _____

10 How many minutes are there in 20 hours? _____

Key

600	S	1,240	M	900	E
420	C	120	D	450	B
1,200	N	180	X	1,100	I
660	S	300	A	240	A
1,080	T	60	L	360	O

Where does a king stay when he goes to the beach?

A ___ ___ ___ ___   ___ ___ ___ ___ ___ ___
    6   3 10 2   5   4   7   9   1   8

A Riddle to Dive Into

Answer each question.

To solve the riddle, find the question number at the bottom of the page.

Then, use your answers and the Decoder to fill in the blanks.

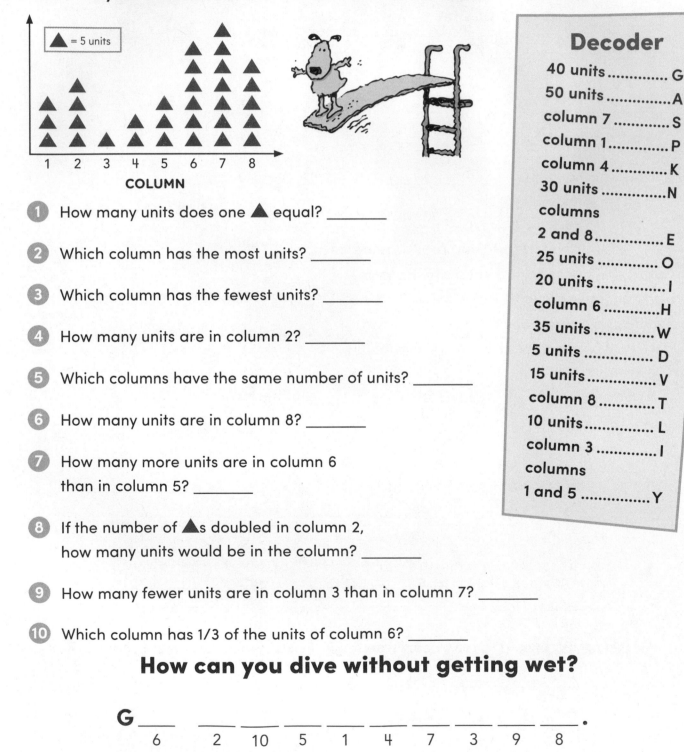

Decoder

40 units .... G

50 units .... A

column 7 .... S

column 1 .... P

column 4 .... K

30 units .... N

columns
2 and 8 .... E

25 units .... O

20 units I

column 6 .... H

35 units .... W

5 units .... D

15 units V

column 8 .... T

10 units L

column 3 I

columns
1 and 5 .... Y

1 How many units does one ▲ equal? _____

2 Which column has the most units? _____

3 Which column has the fewest units? _____

4 How many units are in column 2? _____

5 Which columns have the same number of units? _____

6 How many units are in column 8? _____

7 How many more units are in column 6
than in column 5? _____

8 If the number of ▲s doubled in column 2,
how many units would be in the column? _____

9 How many fewer units are in column 3 than in column 7? _____

10 Which column has 1/3 of the units of column 6? _____

How can you dive without getting wet?

G ___ ___ ___ ___ ___ ___ ___ ___ ___ ___ .
   6   2 10 5   1   4   7   3   9   8

How's Your Heart Rate?

Materials:
• stopwatch or watch with a second hand
• tennis ball

Each day your heart beats about 100,000 times. That's enough times to pump almost 1,500 gallons of blood throughout your body! By the time you are 70 years old, your heart will have pumped about 38 million gallons of blood. No wonder it's important to keep your heart strong and healthy!

The number of times a heart beats in a certain amount of time is called heart rate. Check out the table to find some average animal heart rates. Then, follow the steps to add your heart rate to the table.

How to Find Your Heart Rate
• **Place two fingers on your neck or your wrist. Move them around until you feel a pulse beat.**
• **Count the beats for 30 seconds. Have a partner time you with the watch.**
• **Multiply the number of beats by 2. That number is your heart rate for 1 minute.**

ANIMAL	HEART RATE (for one minute)
Canary	1,000
Mouse	650
Chicken	200
Cat	110
Dog	80
Adult human	72
Giraffe	60
Tiger	45
Elephant	25
Gray whale	8
You	

Answer these questions about animals' heart rates, using the information on the table.

1 Which animal's heart beats fastest in 1 minute? _____

Which beats slowest? _____

2 What do you notice about the size of the animal compared with its heart rate?

_____

3 Where do you think a horse's heart rate might fit on the table? Explain your answer.

_____

4 Which animal is your heart rate the closest to? _____

Sampling Cereal

Materials:
- box of alphabet cereal
- measuring cup
- pencil and paper

Are there more Ps than Qs in a box of letter-shaped cereal? How about the other letters? You could look at every piece of cereal in the box. But that could take a while. It might be dinnertime before you get to eat breakfast!

We've got a better idea. Take a sample. A sample is a small part of a larger group. Studying a sample can tell you a lot about the whole group. If you look at the letters in a small bowl of cereal, you can get a good idea about what's in the rest of the box. That leaves only one more thing to figure out: who gets to eat the last bowl!

What to Do:

1   Measure out 1 cup of letter-shaped cereal. This is your sample.

2   Pick 1 piece of cereal out of the cup. Then, make a mark on the tally chart next to the correct letter.

3   Do this for all of the cereal in your sample cupful. Don't count broken pieces. (If you find more than one of the same letter, just mark it again on your tally sheet like this: ||||| ||.)

4   Which letters have the most tally marks on your sheet?

_____

_____

TALLY CHART

A: _____
B: _____
C: _____
D: _____
E: _____
F: _____
G: _____
H: _____
I: _____
J: _____
K: _____
L: _____
M: _____
N: _____
O: _____
P: _____
Q: _____
R: _____
S: _____
T: _____
U: _____
V: _____
W: _____
X: _____
Y: _____
Z: _____

Decibel Tester

A bar graph is used to compare information. This bar graph shows the relative loudness of sound measured in decibels (dB)*. One decibel is the smallest difference between sound heard by the human ear. A 100-decibel sound is 10 times louder than a 10-decibel sound. A 100-decibel sound is painful!

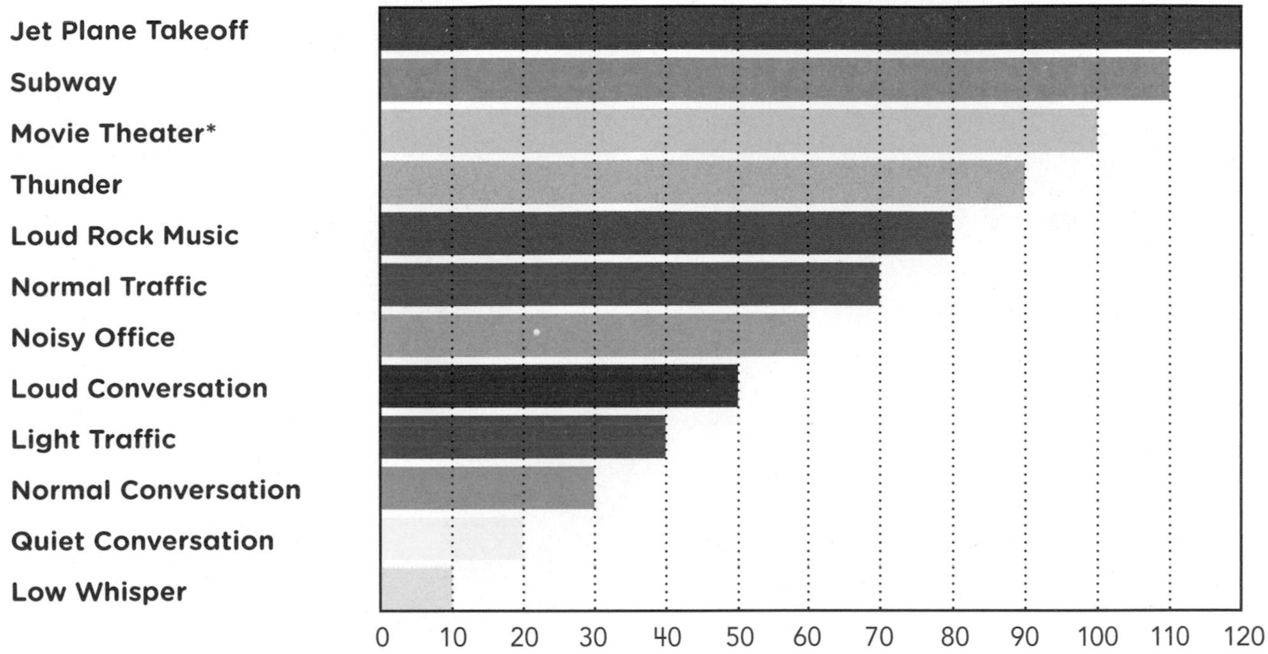

Jet Plane Takeoff
Subway
Movie Theater*
Thunder
Loud Rock Music
Normal Traffic
Noisy Office
Loud Conversation
Light Traffic
Normal Conversation
Quiet Conversation
Low Whisper

0 10 20 30 40 50 60 70 80 90 100 110 120

* Speaker volumes in a digital theater sound system.

1 What is the loudest sound shown on the graph? _____

2 How many decibels is the loudest sound? _____

How much louder in decibels is...

3 Loud conversation than quiet conversation? _____

4 Normal traffic than light traffic? _____

5 A movie theater digital sound system than loud rock music? _____

6 A subway train than thunder? _____

7 A noisy office than quiet conversation? _____

We All Scream for Bar Graphs!

Vanna Lah owns her own ice cream shop. She sells only two ice cream flavors: Marvelous Mint and Great Grape. But keeping track of how much ice cream she's sold isn't so simple for Vanna. Can you help her out?

Use the information at right to make a double bar graph. Draw two bars above each month on the graph. One bar will show how many gallons of Marvelous Mint Vanna sold. The other will show how many gallons of Great Grape she sold.

Hint: Use two different colors to draw your bars—one for Marvelous Mint, and the other for Great Grape. Don't forget to color in your graph's key, too.

OUR FEATURED FLAVORS:
MARVELOUS MINT! GREAT GRAPE!

Information for Graph:
Gallons Sold Each Month

NOVEMBER
Marvelous Mint: 10 gallons
Great Grape: 8 gallons

DECEMBER
Marvelous Mint: 13 gallons
Great Grape: 12 gallons

JANUARY
Marvelous Mint: 9 gallons
Great Grape: 11 gallons

FEBRUARY
Marvelous Mint: 12 gallons
Great Grape: 12 gallons

KEY
☐ Marvelous Mint
☐ Great Grape

VANNA LAH'S ICE CREAM SALES

Gallons Sold

15
14
13
12
11
10
9
8
7
6
5
4
3
2
1
0

November   December   January   February

Month

Great Game Graph!

The circle graph shows how many hours kids play video games each day. The number of kids shown in each section is out of 100 kids. For example, look at the bottom section. It shows that out of every 100 kids, 29 play video games for 1 hour a day.

Use the graph to answer the questions below.

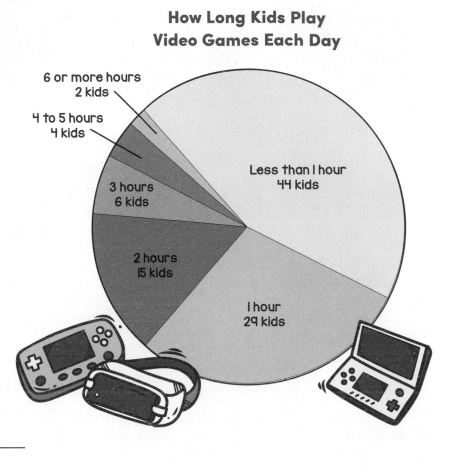

**How Long Kids Play
Video Games Each Day**

6 or more hours
2 kids

4 to 5 hours
4 kids

3 hours
6 kids

2 hours
15 kids

Less than 1 hour
44 kids

1 hour
29 kids

1 How many kids out of 100 play video games for 2 hours a day? _____

2 How many hours a day do 6 out of 100 kids play video games? _____

3 For how long does the largest group of kids play video games each day? _____

4 For how long does the smallest group of kids play video games each day? _____

5 Do more or less than $\frac{1}{2}$ of the kids play video games for less than 1 hour a day?

_____

6 Think of the amount of time you play video games each day. In which section of the

graph would you be? _____

What's Hoppin'?

NOTE: Judy and Rudy can hop in vertical and horizontal directions only.

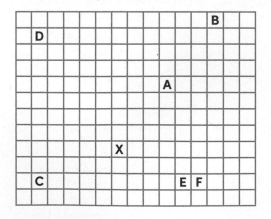

2 Rudy is in square X. Which are the 2 shortest paths he can take to get to square E? _____

You Answer It!

1 Look at the graph below. Starting at square X, Judy hopped 4 squares up and 3 squares to the right. In which square did she land?

_____

3 Judy is in square A. Which are the 2 shortest paths she can take to get to square E? _____

_____

4 Find the 2 shortest paths to get from square X to square D. _____

_____

5 Find 3 paths to get from square D to square E. Does each path contain the same total number of squares? _____

_____

ANSWER KEY

Page 5
1. one 2. ten 3. eight
4. three 5. two 6. hundred
7. nine 8. thousand

Page 6
1. thousands 2. 6 3. tens 4. 7
5. 0 6. billions 7. hundred millions
8. 727,912 9. 4,847,266
10. 7,446,732,011
IN "SCENT"IMETERS

Page 7
1. BARK–RUFF, RUFF–BARK
2. 2 phrases: BARK–GRR, GRR–BARK
3. 6 phrases: MEOW–PURR, MEOW–SSS, PURR–SSS, PURR–MEOW, SSS–PURR, SSS–MEOW
4. 6 phrases: MEOW–PURR–SSS, MEOW–SSS–PURR, PURR–MEOW–SSS, PURR–SSS–MEOW, SSS–PURR–MEOW, SSS–MEOW–PURR

Page 8
1. 800 2. 5,000 3. 3,700 4. 1,000
5. 2,770 6. 8,000 7. 24,400
8. 11,000 9. 9,940 10. 73,000
MILK SHAKES

Page 9
Answers will vary. You might encourage students to keep a list of their moves in order to defend their strategies.

Page 10
1. 100 2. 6,000 3. 1,013
4. 4,247 5. 43,836 6. 15,033
7. 15,068 8. 1,000

Page 11

2	2	4	1			1	9	4	3	
		8		2	7	8		5	8	4	1	1
	1	5	7	8		4	1	1	8		2		3
5	0	2		9		0				2		3
	6			8		2	1	7	2		1	1	6
9			6		6			8		1	
0			5		8		2	3	3	5	
6	7	0	0		1		2		2	9	0	8

Page 12
1. 257 2. 428 3. 300 4. 743
5. 1,451 6. 2,869 7. 459 8. 48
9. 4,884 10. 7,926
"VEGE"TABLES

Page 13
1. 4 x 71 2. 78 x 43 + 1 3. 143 x 8 – 7
4. 18 x 734, or 18 x 743, or 73 x 184, or 74 x 183 5. 418 ÷ 73 or 471 ÷ 83 or 473 ÷ 81 6. 83 ÷ 17

Page 14
1. 6 2. 8 3. 60 4. 63 5. 160
6. 252 7. 90 8. 56 9. 315 10. 96
HE "COMBED" THE TOWN.

Page 15
The only numbers not part of a multiplication number sentence are: 5 [row 1], 9 [row 5], the final 3 [row 6], and 11, 2, and 8 [row 10].

Page 16
1. 11,000 2. 24,000 3. 30,000
4. 56,000 5. 100,000 6. 144,000
7. 210,000 8. 256,000 9. 360,000
10. 375,000
TO CATCH "FLIES"

Page 17
1. 2 2. 5 3. 8 4. 16 5. 3 6. 7
7. 13 8. 4 9. 9
IT'S "TULIPS"!

Page 18
1. 14R4 2. 2R8 3. 10R1 4. 5R5
5. 2R9 6. 3 7. 4R16 8. 9R1
9. 4 10. 8
A BASEBALL TEAM

Page 19
1. 56 2. 84 3. 95 4. 301
5. 250 6. 267

Page 20
1. 4 2. 20 R10 3. 11 4. 6 R58
5. 9 R7 6. 9 R50 7. 5 8. 33 R12
9. 30 R40 10. 30 R23
A YARDSTICK

Page 21
1. 29 2. 10 3. 22 4. 60
5. Answers will vary.

Page 22

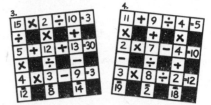

Page 23
1. 1/3 2. 3/8 3. 3/11 4. 14/20
5. 1/32 6. 20/67 7. 59/83 8. 22/121
9. 3/156 10. 99/312
"YOU ATTRACT ME."

Page 24
1. 3/2 2. 5/3 3. 2/6 4. 8/5 5. 9/4
6. 14/8 7. 36/9 8. 10/3 9. 16/7
10. 54/11
HE PAINTED BY NUMBERS.

Page 25
1. 0.6 2. 0.4 3. 0.42 4. 2.6 5. 2.6
6. 0.22 7. 0.25 8. 0.07 9. 3.2
10. 0.75 11. 4.6 12. 0.008
SO IT WON'T PEEL.

Page 26
The correct ranking from highest to lowest is:
1–Miguel Cabrera (.338)
2–Dee Strange-Gordon (.333)
3–Bryce Harper (.330)
4–Paul Goldschmidt (.321)
5–Xander Bogaerts (.320)
6–Buster Posey (.318)
7–A. J. Pollock (.315)
8–Yunel Escobar (.314)
9–Joey Votto (.314)
10–José Altuve (.313)

Page 27
186 Elway Electrician
7.2 Alan Architect
20 Carlton Carpenter
3 Paul Plumber
500 Robert Roofer
80 Gilbert Gardener
27 Penny Painter

Page 28
1. 8; 11; 14; 17; 20; 23; 26; 29
2. 27; 29; 31; 33; 35; 37; 39; 41
3. 2; 7; 12; 17; 22; 27; 32; 37; 42
4. 5; 9; 14; 23; 37; 60; 97; 157; 254
5. 39; 46; 53; 60; 67; 74; 81; 88; 95
6. 6; 7; 13; 20; 33; 53; 86; 139; 225
7. 4; 15; 26; 37; 48; 59; 70; 81
8. 93; 116; 209; 325; 534; 859; 1,393; 2,252; 3,645

Page 29
1. zero **2.** times **3.** factor **4.** triple
5. double **6.** product **7.** multiply
8. addition **9.** same size
Unscrambled word: multiples
Definitions will vary.

Page 30
1. 12 **2.** 8 **3.** 9 **4.** 31 **5.** 60 **6.** 36, 48

Page 31
1. $6.80, $10.20 **2.** $7.20, $16.80
3. $3.30, $18.70 **4.** $13.00, $52.00

Page 32
1. 3.5, 2.5 **2.** 4.25, 4
3. 0.6, 0.4 **4.** 4.8, 5.8

Page 33
1. 4 apples **2.** 9 books **3.** 25 caps
4. 20 oranges **5.** 30 coats **6.** 18 shoes
7. 56 bananas **8.** 121 pencils
IT CUT A CORNER.

Page 34
1. 1.5 inches
2. 3.2 inches
3. The highest temperature was reached on Sunday. The lowest temperature was reached on Thursday. The difference between the two temperatures was 30 degrees.
4. The temperature dropped 15 degrees between Wednesday and Thursday. The temperature increased by 15 degrees between Saturday and Sunday.
5. 27 degrees

Page 35
1. 6 cones **2.** 5 cups
3. the cup **4.** 5 1/2 drink boxes

Page 36
1. railway signal **2.** ironing board
3. gas mask **4.** cash register
5. ear muffs **6.** ballpoint pen
7. hearing aid **8.** windshield wiper

Page 37
1. Add four crackers (units).

2. The area will be 9.

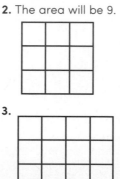

3.

4. Possible answers include: a square 4 units by 4 units with a perimeter of 16, a rectangle 2 units by 8 units with a perimeter of 20, a rectangle 1 unit by 16 units with a perimeter of 34.
5. Answers will vary, but any correct answer will use 24 units.

Page 38
1. 12 **2.** 24 **3.** 48 **4.** 60 **5.** 84
6. 108 **7.** 120 **8.** 72 **9.** 144 **10.** 180
TO GET "CHECKED OUT"

Page 39
1. 60 **2.** 120 **3.** 240 **4.** 300
5. 420 **6.** 600 **7.** 660 **8.** 900
9. 1,080 **10.** 1,200
A SAND CASTLE

Page 40
1. 5 units **2.** column 7 **3.** column 3
4. 20 units **5.** columns 1 and 5
6. 25 units **7.** 15 units **8.** 40 units
9. 30 units **10.** column 4
GO SKYDIVING.

Page 41
1. The canary's heart rate is the fastest. The gray whale's heart rate is the slowest.
2. Answers may vary. In general, the smaller the animal, the faster the heart rate.
3. A horse's heart beats 25–40 times per minute. It would fit between the elephant and the tiger. That answer would be logical because a horse is larger than a tiger but smaller than an elephant.
4. Answers will vary.

Page 42
4. Answers will vary.

Page 43
1. Jet plane takeoff **2.** 120 dB
3. 30 dB **4.** 30 dB **5.** 20 dB
6. 20 dB **7.** 40 dB

Page 44
Students' graphs should represent the sale of the two flavors for the four months given.

Page 45
1. 15 kids **2.** 3 hours a day
3. Less than 1 hour a day
4. 6 or more hours a day
5. Less than 1/2 **6.** Answers will vary.

Page 46
1. Judy landed in square A.
2. Down 2 squares and 4 squares to the right; 4 squares to the right and down 2 squares
3. 1 square to the right and 6 squares down; 6 squares down and 1 square to the right
4. 7 squares up and 5 squares to the left; 5 squares to the left and 7 squares up
5. Answers will vary. Each path does not have to have the same number of squares.